D0536983

FLOWERS

TULIPS

John F. Prevost
ABDO & Daughters

Published by Abdo & Daughters, 4940 Viking Drive, Suite 622, Edina, Minnesota 55435.

Copyright © 1996 by Abdo Consulting Group, Inc., Pentagon Tower, P.O. Box 36036, Minneapolis, Minnesota 55435 USA. International copyrights reserved in all countries. No part of this book may be reproduced in any form without written permission from the publisher.

Printed in the United States.

Cover Photo credits: Peter Arnold, Inc.
Interior Photo credits: Peter Arnold, Inc.

Edited by Bob Italia

Library of Congress Cataloging-in-Publication Data

Prevost, John F.
    Tulips / John F. Prevost.
    p. cm. -- (Flowers)
    Includes index.
    Summary: Describes the tulip flower, and varieties of tulips, the bulbs and seeds, and the various insect pests and diseases that may attack these popular spring flowering bulbs.
    ISBN 1-56239-612-9
    1. Tulips--Juvenile literature. [1. Tulips.] I. Title. II. Series: Prevost, John F.
    Flowers
    QK495.L72P725 1996
    584' .324--dc20
                                       96-1338
                                            CIP
                                            AC

Contents

Tulips and Family

Tulips are one of the most common spring flowering **bulbs**. They may be planted indoors to **blossom** during the winter or outside to flower in a yard, garden, or planter.

Tulip flowers come in many colors, including white, red, yellow, blue, or black. Some **varieties** have cuplike, fringed, or even roselike flowers.

Tulips first appeared in Asia. There are more than 100 types, all of which belong to the lily family.

Merchants brought tulips to the Netherlands more than 400 years ago. By 1600, the country was the center of tulip production. Because they were popular, tulips became expensive. Today, anyone can buy and grow these beautiful flowers.

Tulips have a wide range of colors and patterns.

Roots, Soil, and Water

Tulips grow year after year from their **bulbs**. Bulbs store food that allow plants to survive through the winter.

A tulip bulb has a thin brown skin called a **tunic**. This surrounds **scales**—types of leaves that store plant food. Scales make up most of the bulb.

At the bottom of the bulb are the roots. The roots find and collect water, **minerals,** and other **nutrients** that help the plant grow.

Tulips live in dry areas. Some grow well in **fertile** soil, but will rot if they get too wet. Many tulips also grow on rocky, mountain slopes in Asia.

A tulip bulb.

Stems, Leaves, and Sunlight

The tulip's leaves and stems grow above ground. There, the plant captures sunlight to make food.

The leaves combine this sunlight with water, air, **minerals,** and other **nutrients** to make food. This process is called **photosynthesis.**

The food then travels back to the **bulb** and roots. The bulb scales store some of the food, which the tulip feeds on while it is **dormant**.

The stems support the flowers and leaves. They raise the **blossoms** above the leaves so insects can **pollinate** the flowers. In some tulips, the leaves grow from a stem below the ground.

Photosynthesis

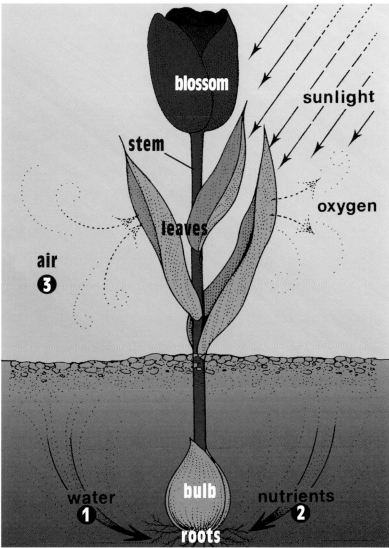

Ground water (1) and nutrients (2) travel through the roots and stems and into the leaves where air (3) is drawn in. Then the plant uses sunlight to change these three elements into food and oxygen.

9

Flowers

Tulip flowers come in a rainbow of colors. There are single and multi-colored **varieties**.

The flower shapes also differ. There are simple cup-shaped **blossoms**, lily-flowered tulips with pointed **petals**, and a variety of frilled- and split-petaled flowers. There may be one or more flowers on a stem, which can be long or short.

There are three main parts to a tulip flower: the petal, the **stamen,** and the **pistil**. The petals are the showy part of the flower. They are small leaves that protect the flower and attract insects with their color. The stamen makes pollen which fertilizes the pistil's **ovules**. The **fertilized** ovules develop into seeds.

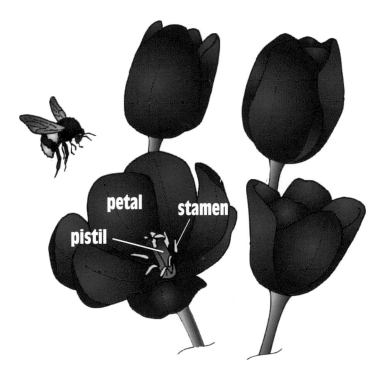

The main parts of the tulip are the petal, pistil, and stamen. The stamen makes pollen that fertilizes the pistil's ovules. The ovules then grow into seeds.

Seeds

Tulip seeds grow in the flower's **ovary** chambers. As the seeds ripen, the chambers form **capsules**. When ripe, the capsules split and release tiny seeds. The dry capsules are the tulip's fruit.

Each seed contains a tulip **embryo**. There is enough food within the seed to allow the tiny plant to grow. After sprouting, it may take six years before the plants flower.

Most people plant tulip **bulbs**. Tulips also grow smaller bulbs from the main bulb.

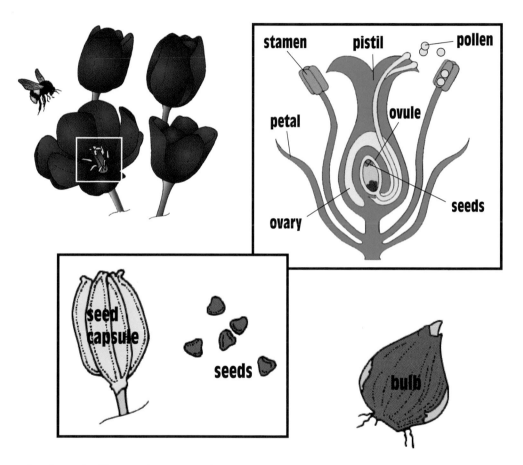

As the pistil's ovules grow into seeds, the ovary forms a capsule. The capsule protects the seeds until they are ripe. Each seed contains a tiny plant embryo which will one day grow into a tulip plant.

Insects and Other Friends

Tulips have colorful flowers to attract **pollinating** insects. Bees, butterflies, wasps, and other insects carry **pollen** from flower to flower. Without the help of these insects, tulips could not **reproduce** with seeds. Flower **nectar** rewards the insects with a small meal.

Spiders, ladybugs, and other **predators** are also attracted to tulips. They seek **prey** by hiding in or around the leaves and **petals**. These predators help the tulip by eating harmful **pests**.

Insects often live within the colorful flowers of the tulip.

Pests and Diseases

Aphids, caterpillars, and beetles eat tulips as the plants lie **dormant** in the ground or grow in the spring. **Poison** is used to fight these pests.

Not all **pests** are insects. Deer, squirrels, and rabbits will eat the **bulbs**, leaves, and flowers.

Diseases also attack tulip leaves and **petals** with a brown **decay**. Too much water, damage during planting, or improper storage before planting also invite deadly diseases.

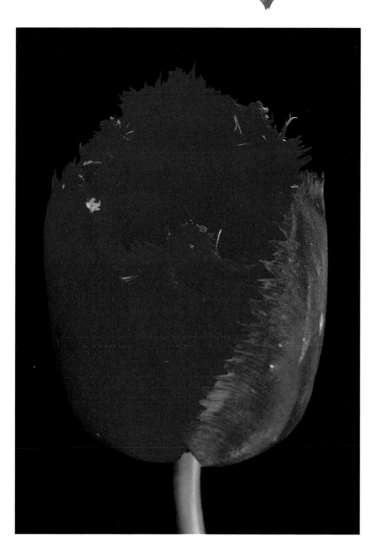

Diseases affect the leaves and petals of tulips.

Varieties

There are more than 100 kinds of tulips in the world. They are found mostly in **temperate** areas of central Asia. More than 5,000 **varieties** are divided into 15 **categories**. Each category separates tulips into different flowering types and times of flowering.

Although tulips are **perennials**, most are planted in the fall for one spring season. Most varieties will not bloom from year to year, so they are replaced.

The many varieties of tulips are found in temperate weather.

Tulips and the Plant Kingdom

The plant kingdom is divided into several groups, including flowering plants, fungi, plants with bare seeds, and ferns.

 Flowering plants grow flowers to make seeds. These seeds often grow inside protective ovaries or fruit.

 Fungi are plants without leaves, flowers, or green coloring, and cannot make their own food. They include mushrooms, molds, and yeast.

 Plants with bare seeds (such as evergreens and conifers) do not grow flowers. Their seeds grow unprotected, often on the scale of a cone.

 Ferns are plants with roots, stems, and leaves. They do not grow flowers or seeds.

There are two groups of flowering plants: monocots (MAH-no-cots) and dicots (DIE-cots). Monocots have seedlings with one leaf. Dicots have seedlings with two leaves.

The lily family is one type of monocot. All tulip varieties are part of the lily family.

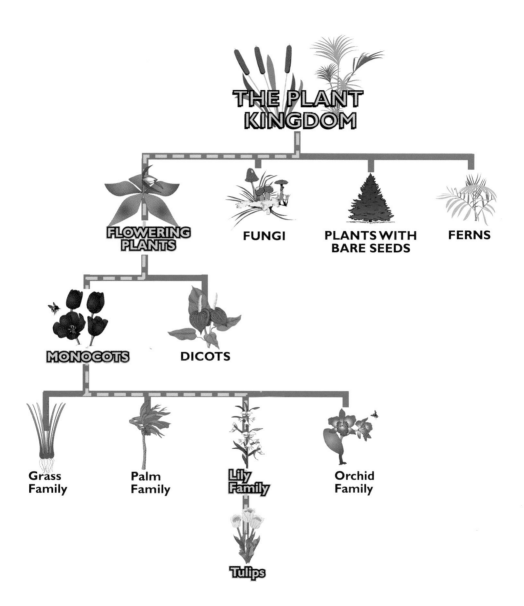

THE PLANT KINGDOM

FLOWERING PLANTS

FUNGI

PLANTS WITH BARE SEEDS

FERNS

MONOCOTS

DICOTS

Grass Family

Palm Family

Lily Family

Orchid Family

Tulips

Glossary

aphid (AY-fid) - A small insect that sucks sap from plant leaves and stems.

blossom (BLAH-sum) - The flower of a plant.

bulb - A short, underground stem used for food storage.

capsule (CAP-sool) - The flower part that holds the seeds.

category (KAT-uh-gor-ee) - A group of things.

decay (de-KAY) - To become rotten.

disease (diz-EEZ) - A sickness.

dormant (DOOR-mant) - The state of resting or inactivity.

embryo (EM-bree-oh) - The early stage of plant development, before sprouting from a seed.

fertile (FUR-tul) - Rich in material needed for plant growth.

fertilize (FUR-tuh-lies) - To develop the ovule into a seed.

merchant (MIR-chant) - A person who buys and sells goods for a living.

mineral - Any substance that is not a plant, animal, or other living thing.

nectar - A sweet fluid found in some flowers.

nutrients (NEW-tree-ents) - Substances that help a plant grow and stay healthy.

ovary (OH-vah-ree) - The part of the flower where seeds grow.

ovule (AH-vule) - A seed before it is fertilized by pollen.

perennial (purr-EN-ee-ull) - A plant that lives for three or more years.

pest - A harmful or destructive insect.

petal - One of several leaves that protect the center of a flower.

photosynthesis (foe-toe-SIN-tuh-sis) - The use of sunlight to make food.

pistil (PIS-til) - The female (seed-making) flower part.

poison - A substance that is dangerous to life or health.

pollinate (PAHL-ih-nate) - The use of pollen to fertilize a flower.

predator (PRED-uh-tore) - An animal that eats other animals.

prey (PRAY) - An animal hunted for food.

reproduce (re-pro-DUCE) - To produce offspring.

scales - Types of leaves that store food.

stamen (STAY-men) - The male flower part (the flower part that makes pollen).

temperate (TEM-prit) - Not very hot and not very cold.

tunic (TOO-nik) - The thin, brown skin of the tulip bulb.

varieties (vuh-RYE-uh-tees) - Different types of plants that are closely related.

Index

A

Asia 4, 6, 18

B

bees 14
blossom 4, 8, 10
bulbs 4, 6, 8, 12, 16
butterflies 14

C

capsule 12
color 10, 14, 20
cone 20

D

decay 16
dicots 20
disease 16

E

embryo 12

F

fall 18
ferns 20
fertilization 10
flowering plants 20
flowers 4, 8, 10, 12, 14,
    16, 18, 20
food 6, 8, 12, 20
fruit 12, 20
fungi 20

G

garden 4
ground 8, 16

I

insects 8, 10, 14, 16

L

leaves 6, 8, 10, 14, 16,
    20
lilies 4, 10
lily family 20

M

minerals 6, 8
molds 20
monocots 20
mountain slopes 6
mushrooms 20

N

nectar 14
nutrients 6, 8

O

ovaries 12, 20
ovules 10

P

perennials 18
pests 14, 16
petals 10, 14, 16
photosynthesis 8
pistil 10
plant kingdom 20
planter 4
planting 16
pollen 10, 14
pollinating insects 8
pollination 14

R

predator 14
prey 14

R

reproduction 14
roots 6, 8, 20

S

scales 6, 8
seedlings 20
seeds 10, 12, 14, 20
shapes 10
skin 6
soil 6
spring 18
sprout 12
stamen 10
stems 8, 10, 20
sunlight 8

T

tunic 6

V

varieties 4, 10, 18

W

water 6, 8, 16
winter 4, 6

Y

yeast 20

24